2

All Black Flexing Tour Bus

ESC Key Filter System;

A Blanket E-Scooter

COPYRIGHT

Copyright © Ayvan. All Right Reserved, Copyright © Frederic Coomes and Matthew Empringham, Copyright © Marius Uhlig, Copyright © Robert Smith

Published in 2023 as 'All Black Flexing Tour Bus ESC Key Filter System; A Blanket E-Scooter' by Frederic Coomes and Matthew Empringham.

First edition of 150 published in United Kingdom by Ayvan.

Ayvan is a trademark of Cameron Bensimon, registered in the U.K. and in other countries. Printed and bound in Paris, France by Picture Perfect.

All rights reserved. No part of this book may be reproduced, stored in a retrieval system, or transmitted in any form or by any means, electronic, mechanical, photocopying, recording, or otherwise, without the prior written permission of the publisher, Ayvan. Ayvan.co

CREDITS

Fashion: Frederic Coomes and Matthew Empringham
Art Direction: Maria Verikas
Graphic Design: Nadine Wetzel
Primary Photography: Marius Uhlig
Ayvan Creative Director: Cameron Bensimon
Words: Robert Smith
Casting: Good Catch
Models: Hannah Vincent and Yuma Nakahama
Cover Image: Marius Uhlig

Special Thanks: Bradley Sharpe, Gianna Dispenza, Alfred Brown LTD, Pentonville Rubbers

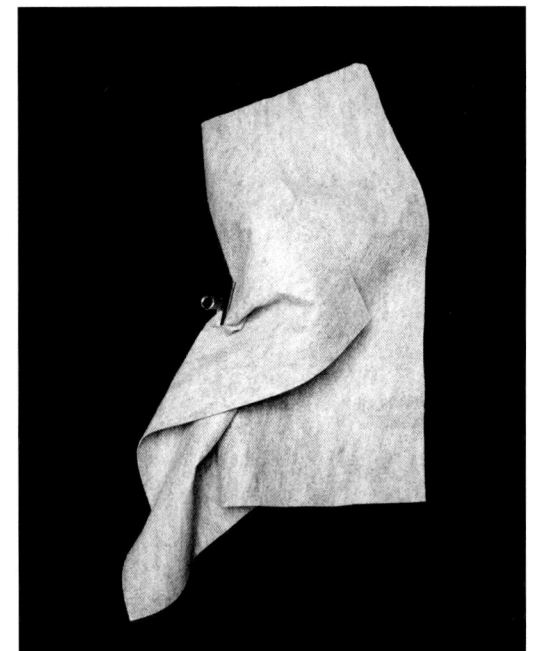

Table of contents

Foreword ... 8

1
ALL BLACK FLEXING TOUR BUS ... 10

T shirt's tshirt	Cotton, Stainless steel	14
"Derelicte."	Leather	18
Boom like.	Latex	20
:)	Adhesive Leather	22
Herdon	Leather, Felt, Stainless steel	30
How do you think of pink?	Papier-mâché	32
Dangly football look.	leather	34
At the dentist.	Latex, Stainless steel	40
We love blue	Silk	48
Its not quite uh oh	Adhesive Leather	52

2
ESC KEY FILTER SYSTEM; ... 62

Geeked.	Apple MacBook Pro 16"	66
Bourney jhetic mahouven	Felt, Tape	70
Big tubes, white tubes, from the chest.	Foam	72
In regards to chilling	Latex	74
PDF squaf	Leather	84
A very chrome spaceship. The shoes are nice.	Neoprene, Stainless steel	104
Mr Evil	Nylon	108
(58isgreat)	PVC	110
We begin to stare.	Jersey, Stainless steel	112
Chico flores from 54	Wool, Latex	114

3
A BLANKET E-SCOOTER ... 120

Pole Dancey	Lime scooter	124
Maybe an inkblot.	Leather, Foam	134
Beavers	Jersey	136
Its blue, so be quiet.	Silk, Stainless steel	138
A naïve angel dance	Jersey	140
Clips on the floral piece.	Neoprene, Stainless steel	144
Huge grant	Cotton	146
Gas Pedal	Papier-mâché	152
A moat, black and see-through.	Leather, PVC	154
A swan, the acrobat.	A4 paper	162

Garment Index ... 168
Material Index ... 170

Foreword

All looks in 'ALL BLACK FLEXING TOUR BUS ESC KEY FILTER SYSTEM; A BLANKET E-SCOOTER' were assembled and disassembled over a 10-day period. Nothing is sewn, instead the recycled materials are held through rings, tape, magnets, glue, and clips. The construction methods are integral to each look and its ability to remain a temporary act of expression, often with the look being realised intuitively on the model. The work is deliberately designed to evoke a sense of finished/beginning.

The concept of finished/beginning encapsulates a paradox of artistic expression. A cyclical process, it embodies deliberate choice to leave certain elements or aspects uncompleted, whilst simultaneously evoking a profound sense of resolution within the overall composition.

This book is designed to feel quick, a snapshot of collaboration and current taste. The book attempts to summarise perspectives on harmony, technology, and pace. It hopes to be aspirational, and make people think about creation and narratives that are built through dress, writing and photography.

1

All Black Flexing Tour Bus

How pets sign birthday cards

I was stood
          with my eyes closed

 when
          I heard the sound.

It came
from the wall
                    next to my bed.

          I looked
over as it
          had fallen silent,
          the words   'BLOCK HEAD'
                                        written in its centre.   I turned back
                                                                                and began

                                                                                                            to
                                                                                                      go about
                                                                                              the mandatory signs
                                                                                  at
                                                                                  my desk.
Then I felt   the wall
                                                              move
                              behind me   with muffled sound,
                                                                      the vibration

                                                                              pulled my
                                                                                      shoulder blades together
                                                                      before
                              The walls silence   the noise stopped.
                              had become
                                very loud.

                                                                              Not to arouse suspicion…

I crept over to my bed.   Nothing came
          I stayed quiet.   from the wall.

                                                  Then a groan.

"Hello?"
          I asked the wall.
                                                                              Nothing in reply.
                                                                                  I knocked on the wall.
                                                                                      Nothing.
                                                                                          I knocked again –
                                                                              there was nothing, again.

I let my face go limp as
          I thought for a second,

then slapped
                              the wall and
                    pushed it
with both hands.

A
"Yes"
　　left the wall.

"Uhm, well me."
　　Replied the wall.

"I am in this pipe, before the descent."
　　They replied.

"I chose this place;
　　I have chosen
　　　　　my own prison."
　　　　　　　They replied.

"To see where I go next will
　　bring me nothing
　　　but pain,
　　　　I am not sad,
　　　　　　and I am not alone,
I do not fear change."

"I am trying
　　to be in love,
　　　　　maybe,
with even
　　several lives
　　　that I have lived,

　　　　　　and even the ones
　　　　I am yet to have."
Explained the wall.

　　　　　　"Hello!
　　Who is behind there?"
　　　　　　　I asked.

　　　　　　"I don't understand,
　　　　　　why are you in
　　　　　　the wall?"

　　　　　This sounded fatal to me.

"So, this is where
　　　you would like to be,
　　　　　stuck in this wall?
With no one else?"
　　　　　　I spoke.

A trumpet began to play,
　　it wasn't musical,

　　it felt conversational
　　or even tonal.

My chest could feel it.

　　　　"Is that you?"
　　　　　I asked the wall.
　　　　　　There was no reply.

　　　　　　instead
　　　the trumpet began to play
lower and faster notes.

ALL BLACK FLEXING TOURBUS   T shirt's tshirt   Cotton, Stainless steel

ALL BLACK FLEXING TOURBUS   "Derelicte."   **Leather**

ALL BLACK FLEXING TOURBUS   Boom like.   Latex

ALL BLACK FLEXING TOURBUS :)   Adhesive Leather   23

Spec

al kit

ALL BLACK FLEXING TOURBUS   **Herdon**   **Leather, Felt, Stainless steel**

ALL BLACK FLEXING TOURBUS		How do you think of pink?		Papier-mâché		33

ALL BLACK FLEXING TOURBUS **Dangly football look.** **Rubber, Stainless steel** 35

ALL BLACK FLEXING TOURBUS   **At the dentist.**   **Latex, Stainless steel**

42

47

ALL BLACK FLEXING TOURBUS   We love blue   Silk   **49**

ALL BLACK FLEXING TOURBUS   Its not quite uh oh   Adhesive Leather

2

ESC Key Filter System;

To tattoo   **a taxidermy**   **dog.**

To tattoo   **a taxidermy**   **dog.**

Not
   too
      much
          sunshine
          could help that
             thought
              bleed
               over.

Car
   doors
      continue to shut.

      And birds
      continue to fly,

however
   how often
      does someone
         interact with them?

To tattoo
   a taxidermy dog
      would be disturbing,

as
   would catching a bird
      in its flight,

         breaking your
      relationship
of sight and sound,

   to one of touch
   and control.

To
   Then
      Landscape
         Her
         Garden
         .

All relationships
   with humans pan out

   in similar
patterns:

      attachment,
      and narrative.

It creates
   emotional interactions
with   anything,   stories...

   Please, wicker chair,
   don't be a grouping of

wood snakes.

Stories are important.

   Vital.

And
   to tattoo
      ataxidermy dog,
         is not.

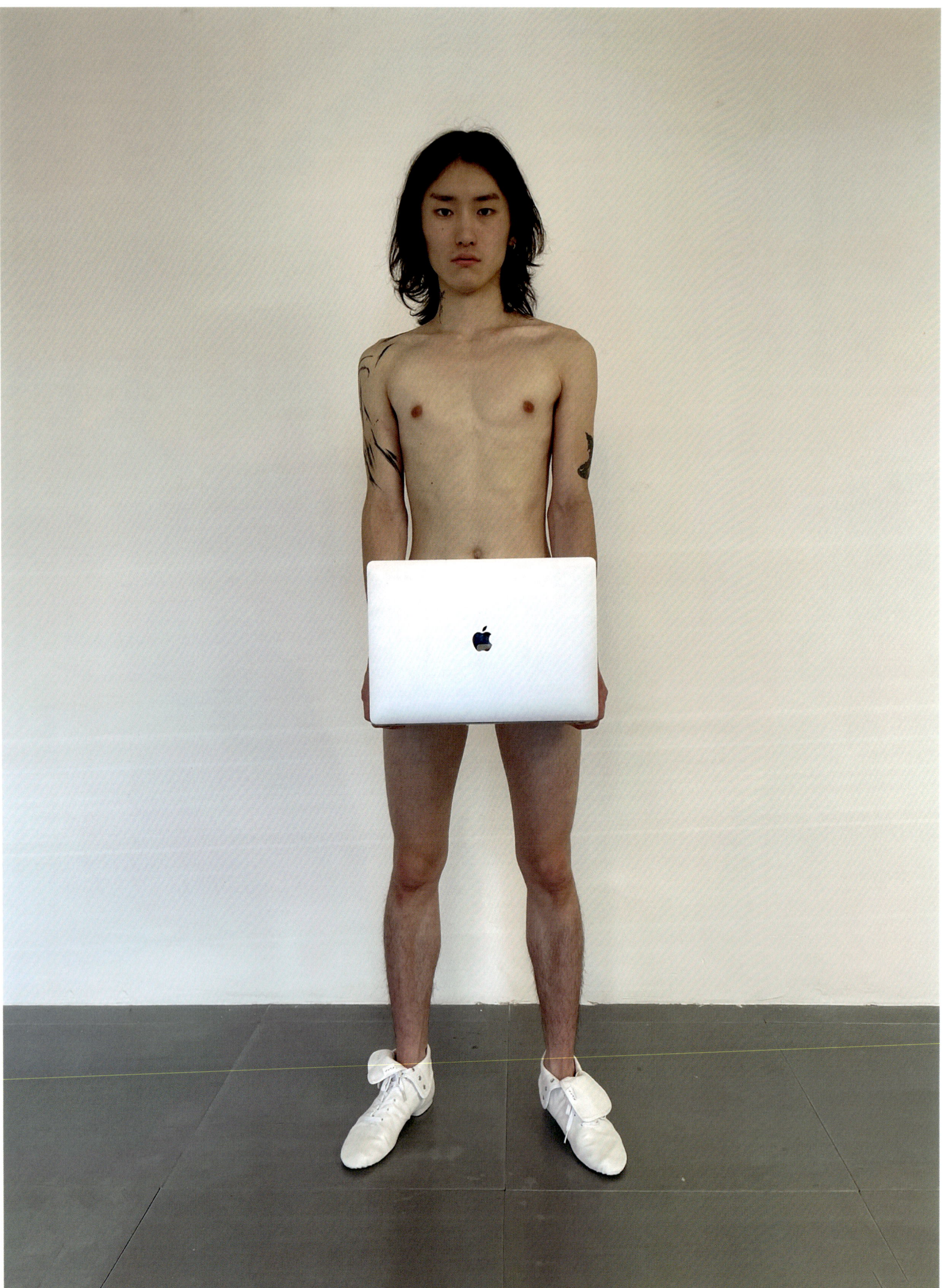

ESC KEY FILTER SYSTEM;   **Bourney jhetic mahouven**   **Felt, Tape**

ESC KEY FILTER SYSTEM;   Big tubes, white tubes, from the chest.   Foam

ESC KEY FILTER SYSTEM; In regards to chilling Latex

PC
SET

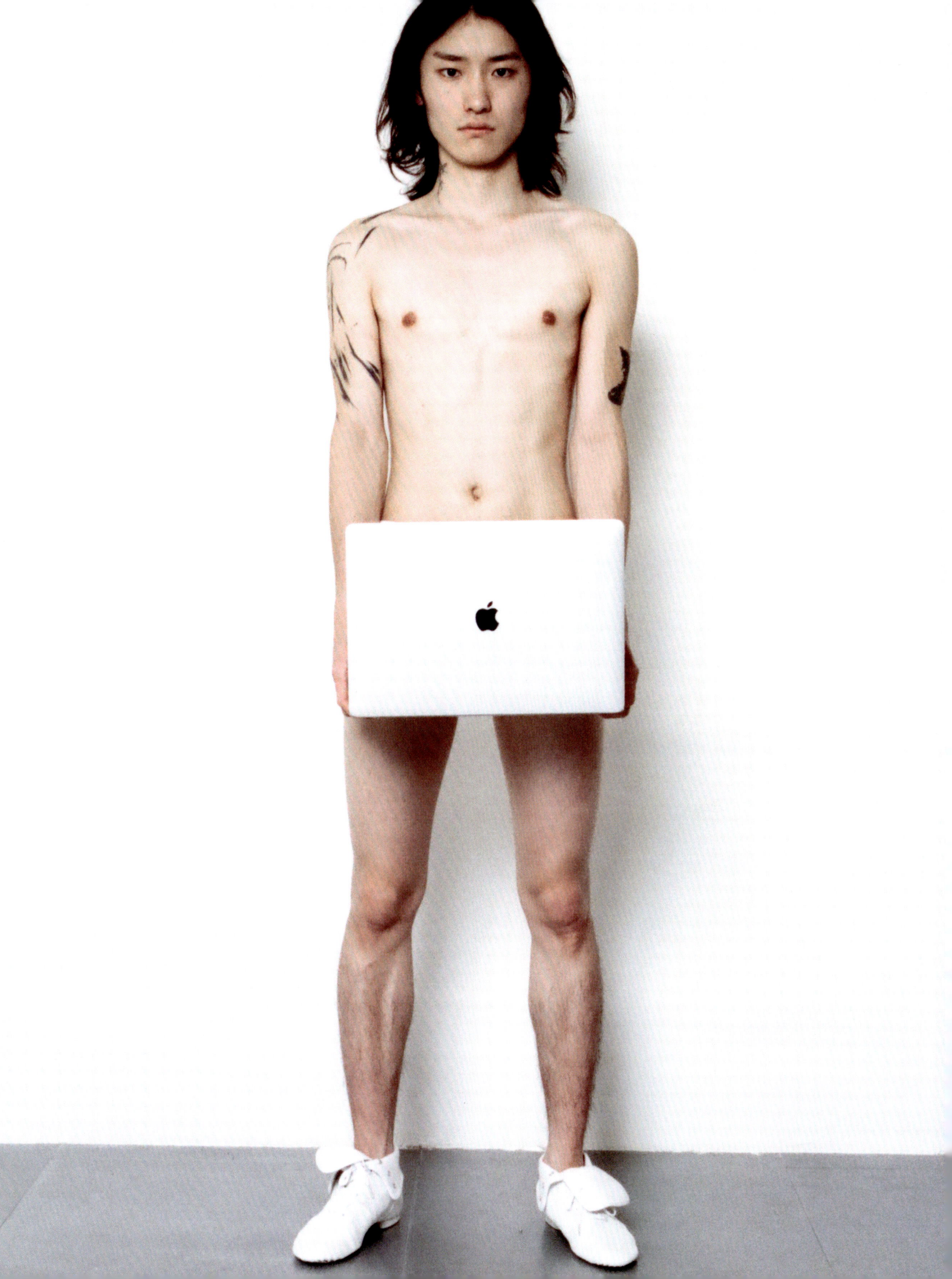

ESC KEY FILTER SYSTEM; PDF squaf Leather

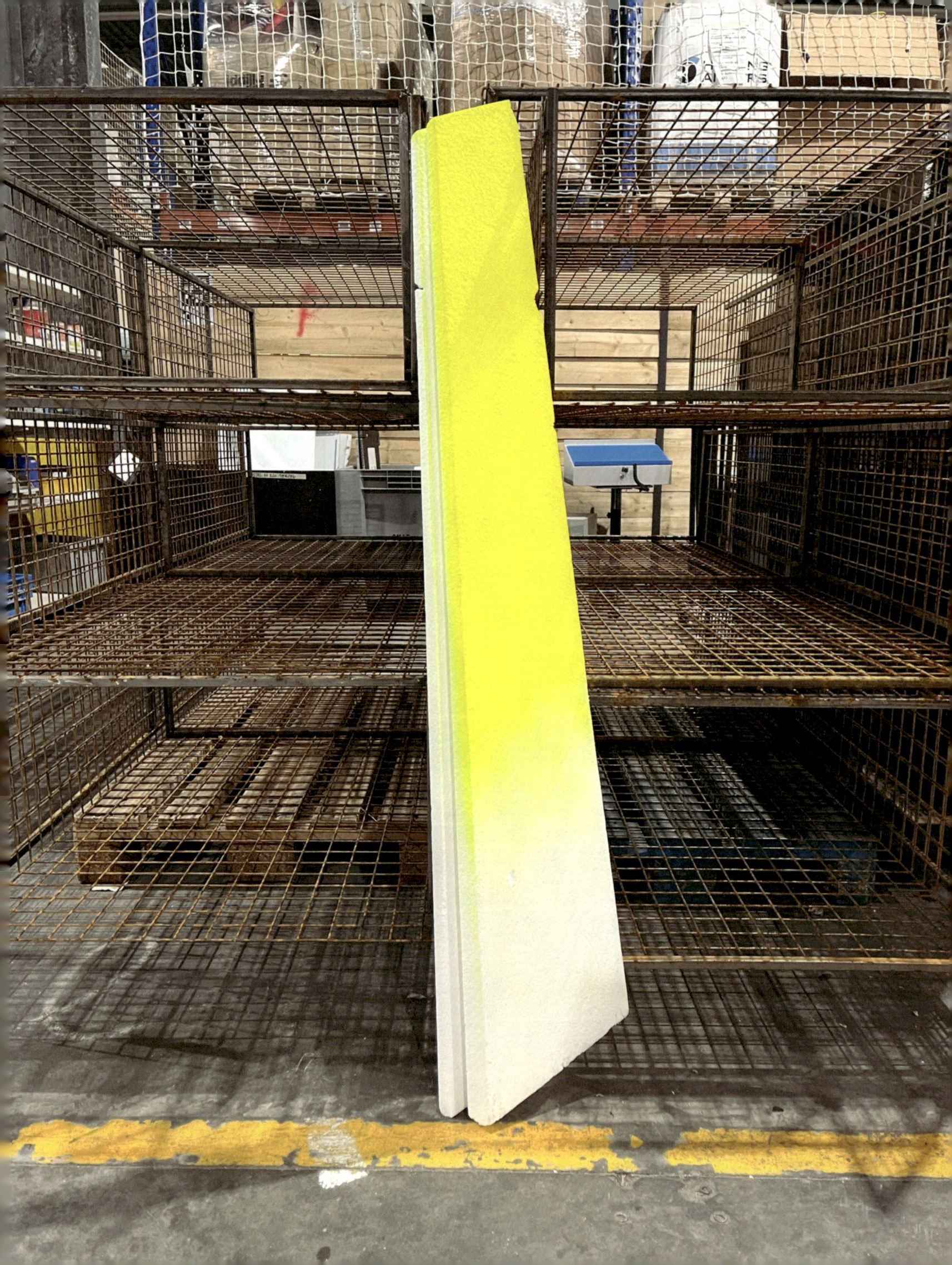

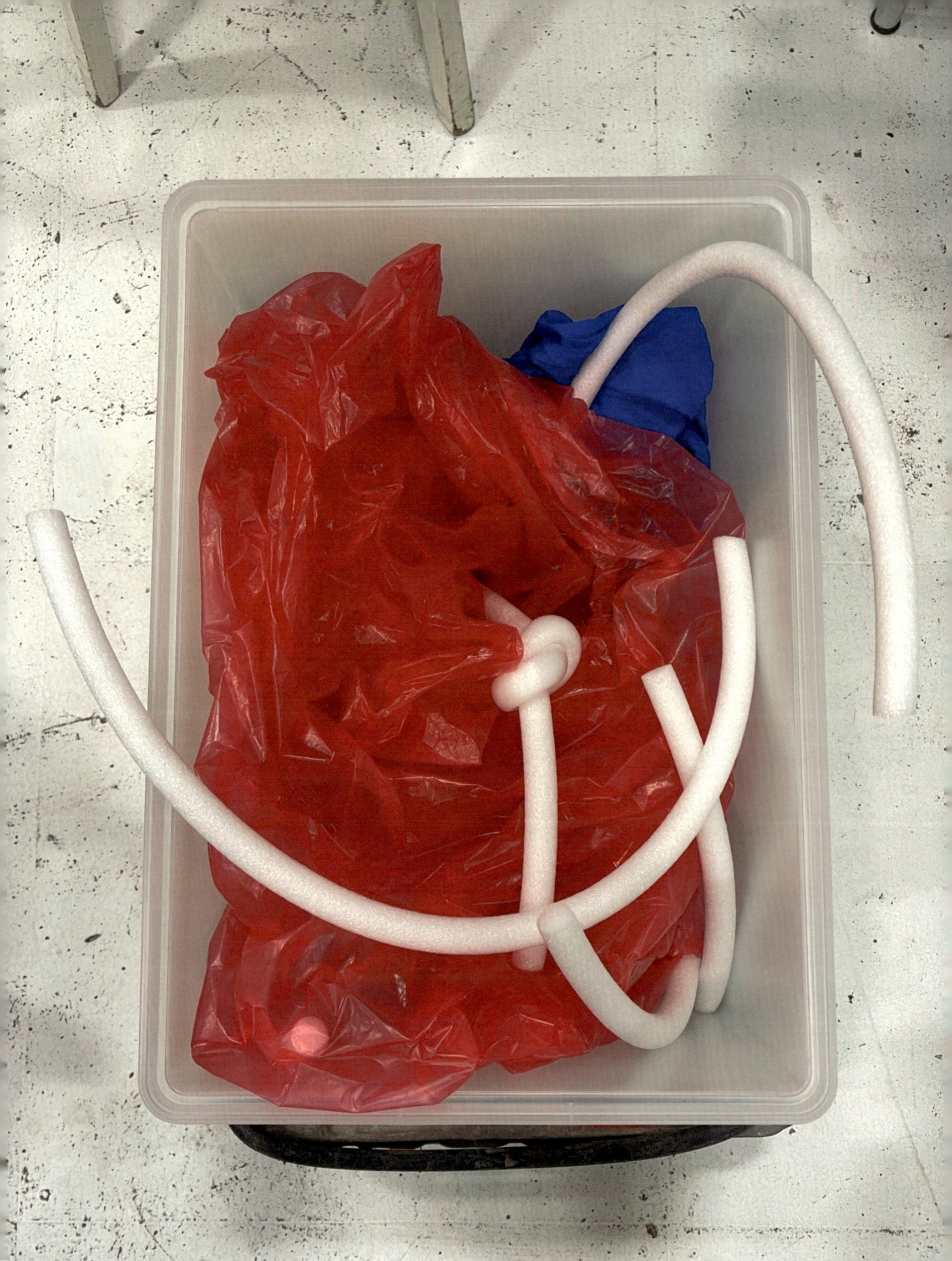

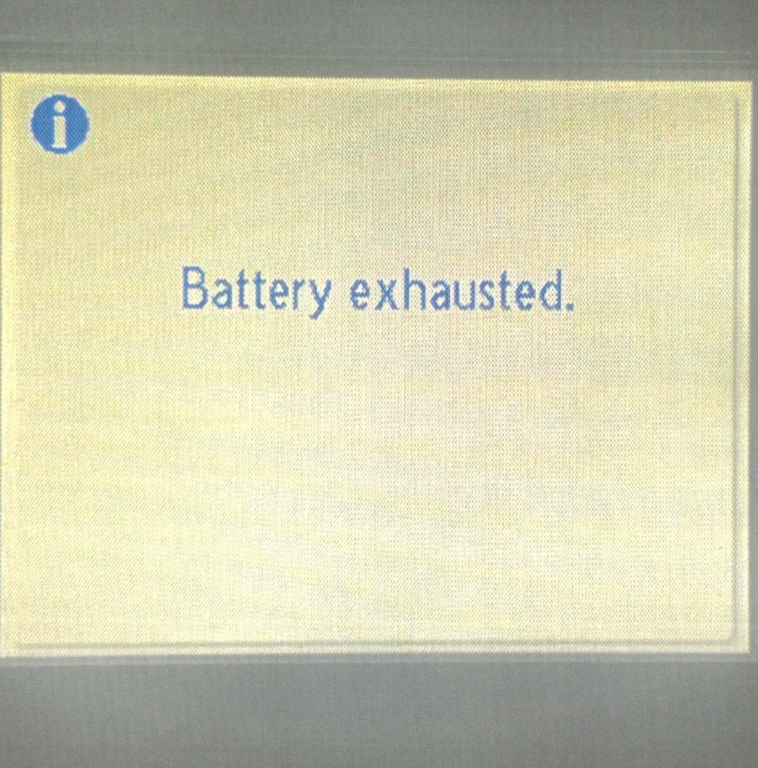

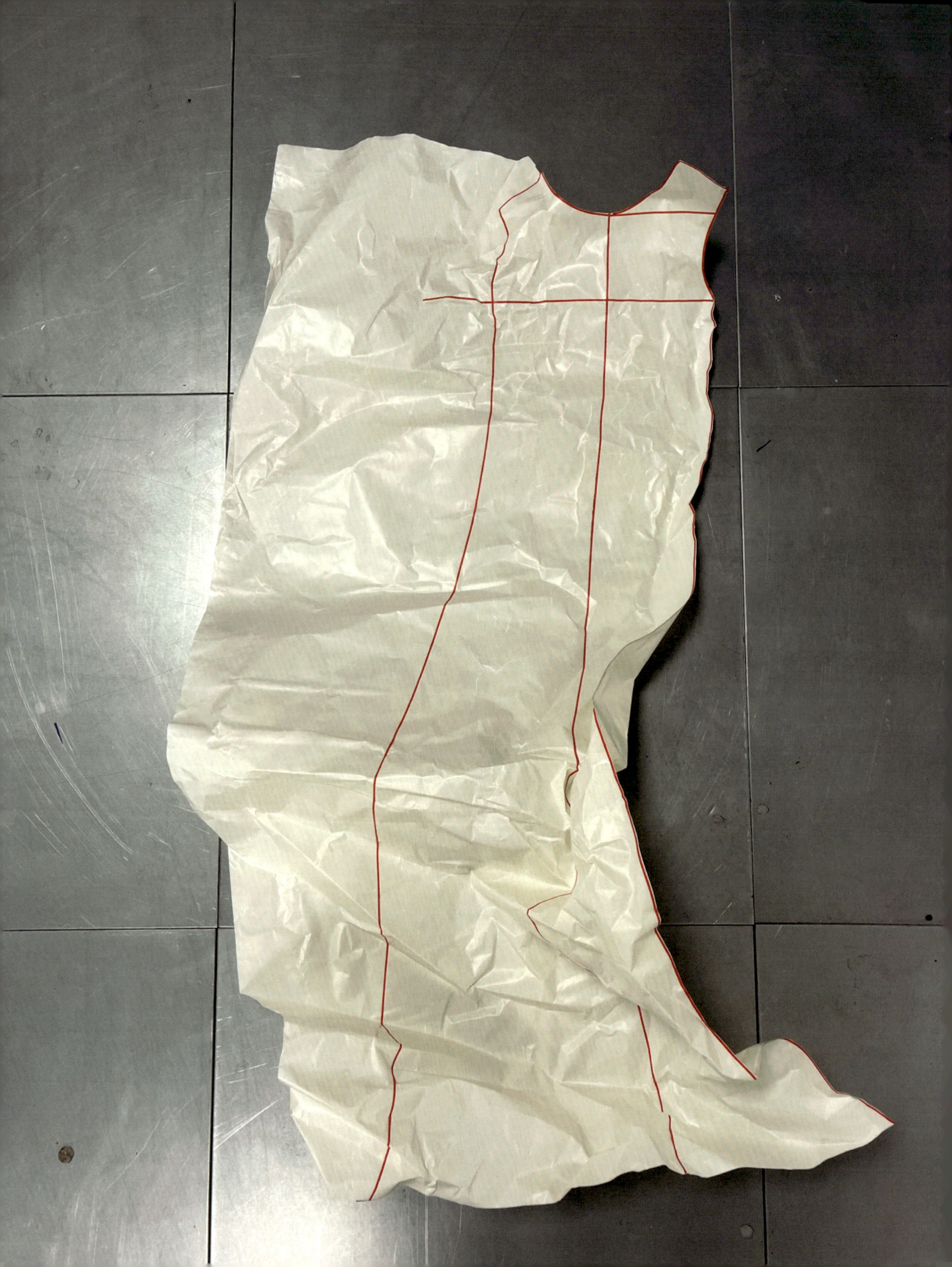

ESC KEY FILTER SYSTEM;   A very chrome spaceship. The shoes are nice.   Neoprene, Stainless steel

ESC KEY FILTER SYSTEM; (58isgreat) PVC 111

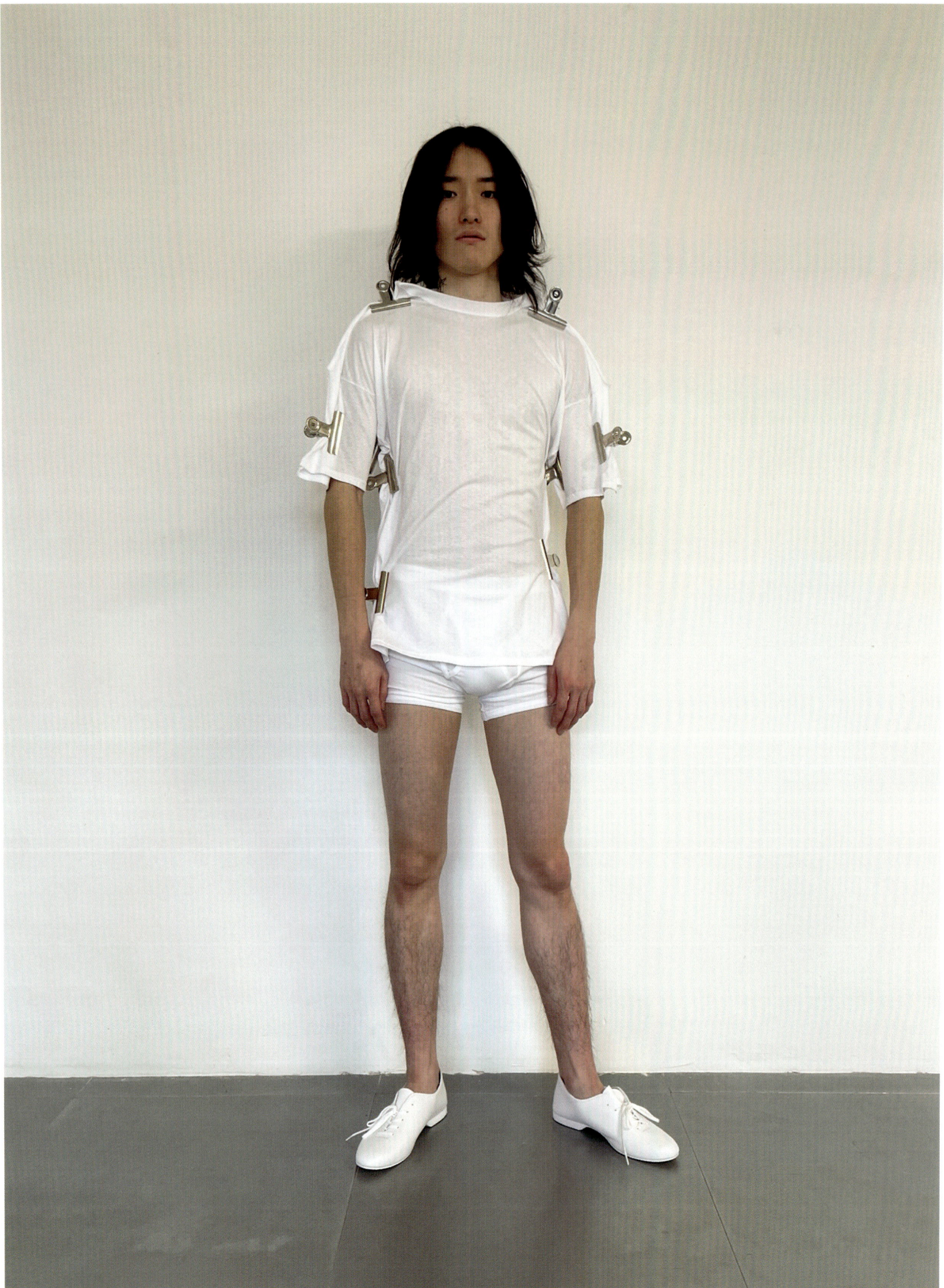

ESC KEY FILTER SYSTEM;   **We begin to stare.**   **Jersey, Stainless steel**   113

ESC KEY FILTER SYSTEM;   **Chico flores from 54**   **Wool, Latex**

Hoo

oodie

3

A Blanket E-Scooter

                                                                                                On the other hand,

                                                                            E-scooters
                                                                                are pretty
                                                                                        popular.
                                    But a blanket
                                        keeps you
                                                                                            Ian Scooter held that
                                                    warm.   one close
                                                                                                        to the chest.
I don't
    know
much   The rubber grips
                                                                                            of the handle bars were nestled

        for scooters
                            and toys.   just
                                                                                    beneath his chin.

The break
         of
           the
              back   Ian Scooter
              wheel   was left handed

just below where   and wore mouth
       his phone lies   tape to sleep.

                        in his left pocket.

                                      The wheels were dirty
                       and had made
                              his blue jeans,
                                      dirty.   Ian Scooter,
                                                          otherwise known
                                                     as 'E' Scooter,
                                                            to closer friends,
                                              was not a wet blanket.

                                                     And he was famous for
                                              playing the trumpet

                                                                    incorrectly.

A BLANKET E-SCOOTER   **Pole Dancey**   **Lime scooter**

ENE
FOC

RGY
JS

A BLANKET E-SCOOTER   **Maybe an inkblot.**   **Leather, Foam**

A BLANKET E-SCOOTER Its blue, so be quiet. Silk, Stainless steel 139

A BLANKET E-SCOOTER　　　　　　　　　　　**A naïve angel dance**　　　　　　　　　　　**Jersey**

A BLANKET E-SCOOTER Clips on the floral piece. Neoprene, Stainless steel

A BLANKET E-SCOOTER Huge grant Cotton

A–Z

A BLANKET E-SCOOTER   Gas Pedal   Papier-mâché

| A BLANKET E-SCOOTER | A moat, black and see-through. | Leather, PVC |

| A BLANKET E-SCOOTER | A swan, the acrobat. | A4 paper | 163 |

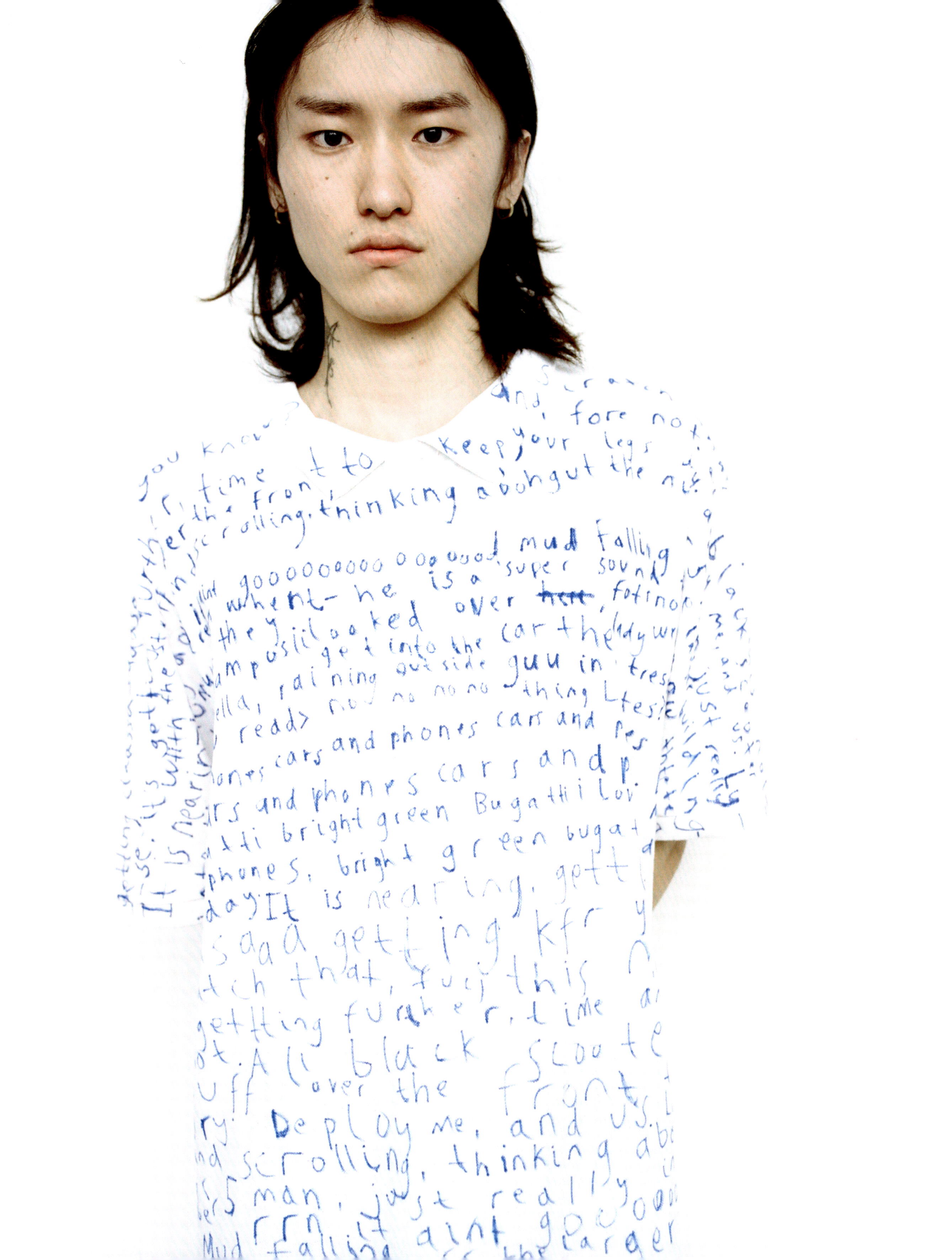

Index

GARMENT INDEX

01
T shirt's tshirt

02
"Derelicte."

03
Boom like.

04
:)

05
Herdon

06
How do you think of pink?

07
Dangly football look.

08
At the dentist.

09
We love blue

10
Its not quite uh oh

11
Geeked.

12
Bourney jhetic mahouven

13
Big tubes, white tubes, from the chest.

14
In regards to chilling

15
PDF squaf

16
A very chrome spaceship. The shoes are nice.

17
Mr Evil

18
(58isgreat)

19
We begin to stare.

20
Chico flores from 54

21
Pole Dancey

22
Maybe an inkblot.

23
Beavers

24
Its blue, so be quiet.

25
A naïve angel dance

26
Clips on the floral piece.

27
Huge grant

28
Gas Pedal

29
A moat, black and see-through.

30
A swan, the acrobat.

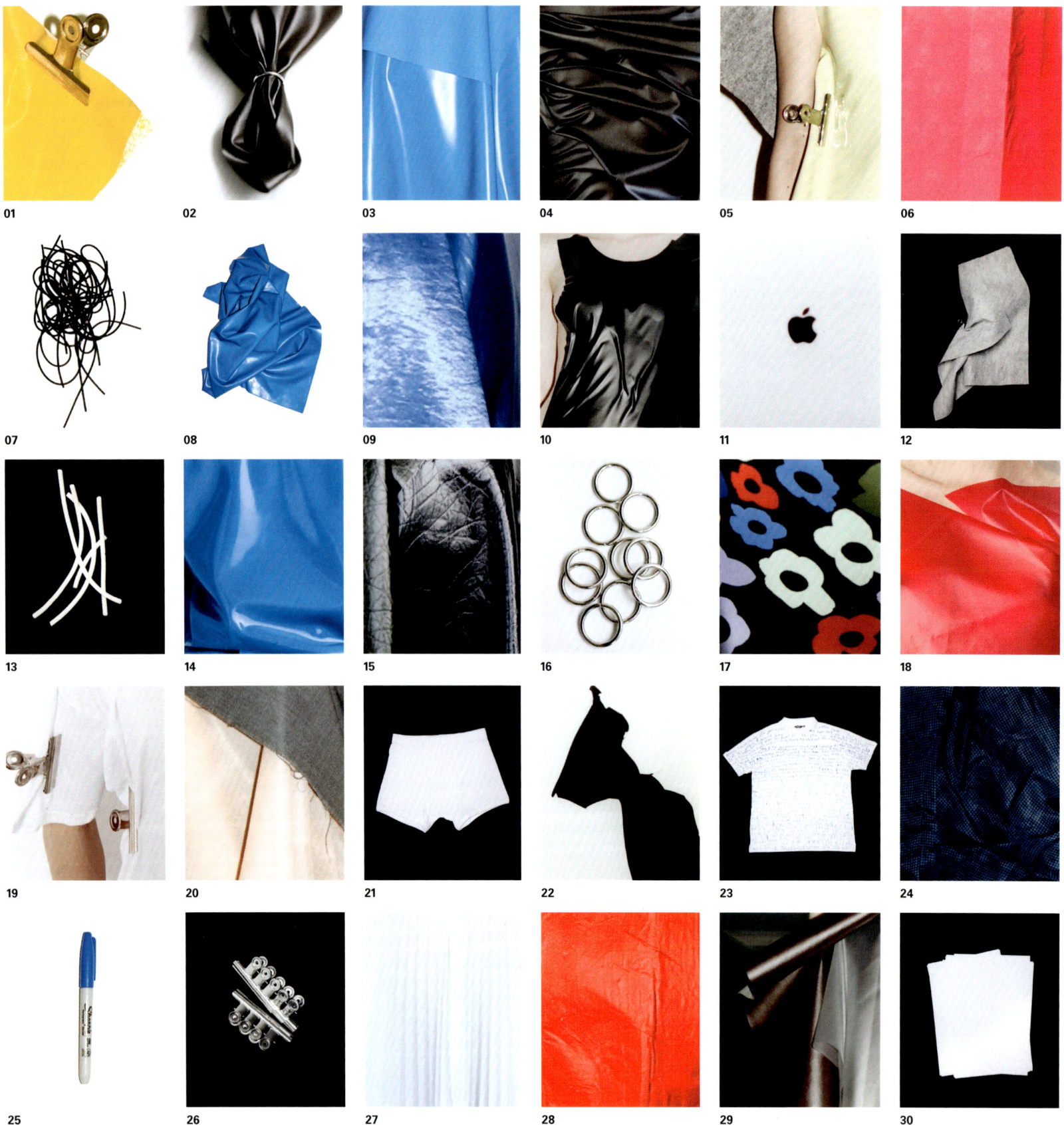

MATERIAL INDEX

01 Cotton, Stainless steel	02 Leather	03 Latex	04 Adhesive Leather	05 Leather, Felt, Stainless steel	06 Papier-mâché
07 Rubber, Stainless steel	08 Latex, Stainless steel	09 Silk	10 Adhesive Leather	11 Apple MacBook Pro 16"	12 Felt, Tape
13 Foam	14 Latex	15 Leather	16 Neoprene, Stainless steel	17 Nylon	18 PVC
19 Jersey, Stainless steel	20 Wool, Latex	21 Lime scooter	22 Leather, Foam	23 Jersey	24 Silk, Stainless steel
25 Jersey	26 Neoprene, Stainless steel	27 Cotton	28 Papier-mâché	29 Leather, PVC	30 A4 paper